SHAKESPEARE'S THE TEMPEST

AN AQA ESSAY WRITING GUIDE

AUTHOR: ASHLEIGH WEIR
SERIES EDITOR: R. P. DAVIS

First published in 2021 by Accolade Tuition Ltd
71-75 Shelton Street
Covent Garden
London WC2H 9JQ
www.accoladetuition.com
info@accoladetuition.com

ISBN 978-1-913988-11-1

FIRST EDITION

1 3 5 7 9 10 8 6 4 2

CONTENTS

EDITOR'S FOREWORD

In your GCSE English Literature exam, you will be presented with an extract from Shakespeare's *The Tempest* and a question that asks you to offer both a close analysis of the extract plus a commentary of the play as a whole. Of course, there are many methods one *might* use to tackle this style of question. However, there is one particular technique which, due to its sophistication, most readily allows students to unlock the highest marks: namely, **the thematic method**.

To be clear, this study guide is *not* intended to walk you through the play scene-by-scene: there are many great guides out there that do just that. No, this guide, by sifting through a series of mock exam questions, will demonstrate *how* to organise a response thematically and thus write a stellar essay: a skill we believe no other study guide adequately covers!

I have encountered students who have structured their essays all sorts of ways: some by writing about the extract line by line, others by identifying various language techniques and giving each its own paragraph. The method I'm advocating, on the other hand, involves picking out three to four themes that will allow you to holistically answer the question: these three to four themes will become the three to four content paragraphs of your essay, cushioned between a brief introduction and conclusion. Ideally, these themes will follow from one to the next to create a flowing argument. Within each of these thematic paragraphs, you can then ensure you are jumping through the mark scheme's hoops.

So to break things down further, each thematic paragraph will include various point-scoring components. In each paragraph, you will quote from the extract, offer analyses of these quotes, then discuss how the specific language techniques you have identified illustrate the theme you're discussing. In each paragraph, you will also discuss how other parts of the play further illustrate the theme (or even complicate it). And in each, you will comment on the era in which the play was written and how that helps to understand the chosen theme.

Don't worry if this all feels daunting. Throughout this guide, Ashleigh (the very talented author!) will be illustrating in great detail – by means of examples – how to build an essay of this kind.

The beauty of the thematic approach is that, once you have your themes, you suddenly have a direction and a trajectory, and this makes essay writing a whole lot

The Shakespearian equivalent of a selfie.

easier. However, it must also be noted that extracting themes in the first place is something students often find tricky. I have come across many candidates who understand the extract and

the play inside out; but when they are presented with a question under exam conditions, and the pressure kicks in, they find it tough to break their response down into themes. The fact of the matter is: the process is a *creative* one and the best themes require a bit of imagination.

In this guide, Ashleigh shall take seven different exam-style questions, coupled with extracts from the play, and put together a plan for each – a plan that illustrates in detail how we will be satisfying the mark scheme's criteria. Please do keep in mind that, when operating under timed conditions, your plans will necessarily be less detailed than those that appear in this volume.

Now, you might be asking whether three or four themes is best. The truth is, you should do whatever you feel most comfortable with: the examiner is looking for an original, creative answer, and not sitting there counting the themes. So if you think you are quick enough to cover four, then great. However, if you would rather do three to make sure you do each theme justice, that's also fine. I sometimes suggest that my student pick four themes, but make the fourth one smaller – sort of like an afterthought, or an observation that turns things on their head. That way, if they feel they won't have time to explore this fourth theme in its own right, they can always give it a quick mention in the conclusion instead.

The Globe Theatre in London. It was built on
the site of the original, which was burnt down in
1613.

Before I hand you over to Ashleigh, I believe it to be worth-
while to run through the four Assessment Objectives the exam
board want you to cover in your response – if only to demonstrate how effective the thematic response can be. I would
argue that the first Assessment Objective (AO1) – the one that
wants candidates to 'read, understand and respond to texts' and
which is worth 12 of the total 34 marks up for grabs – will be
wholly satisfied by selecting strong themes, then fleshing them
out with quotes. Indeed, when it comes to identifying the top-
scoring candidates for AO1, the mark scheme explicitly tells
examiners to look for a 'critical, exploratory, conceptualised
response' that makes 'judicious use of precise references' – the
word 'concept' is a synonym of theme, and 'judicious references' simply refers to quotes that appropriately support the
theme you've chosen.

The second Assessment Objective (AO2) – which is also
responsible for 12 marks – asks students to 'analyse the

language, form and structure used by a writer to create meanings and effects, using relevant subject terminology where appropriate.' As noted, you will already be quoting from the play as you back up your themes, and it is a natural progression to then analyse the language techniques used. In fact, this is far more effective than simply observing language techniques (personification here, alliteration there), because by discussing how the language techniques relate to and shape the theme, you will also be demonstrating how the writer 'create[s] meanings and effects.'

Now, in my experience, language analysis is the most important element of AO2 – perhaps 8 of the 12 marks will go towards language analysis. You will also notice, however, that AO2 asks students to comment on 'form and structure.' Again, the thematic approach has your back – because though simply jamming in a point on form or structure will feel jarring, when you bring these points up while discussing a theme, as a means to further a thematic argument, you will again organically be discussing the way it 'create[s] meanings and effects.'

AO3 requires you to 'show understanding of the relationships between texts and the contexts in which they were written' and is responsible for a more modest 6 marks in total. These are easy enough to weave into a thematic argument; indeed, the theme gives the student a chance to bring up context in a relevant and fitting way. After all, you don't want it to look like you've just shoehorned a contextual factoid into the mix.

Finally, you have AO4 – known also as "spelling and grammar." There are four marks up for grabs here. Truth be told, this guide is not geared towards AO4. My advice? Make sure you are reading plenty of books and articles, because the more you read, the better your spelling and grammar will be. Also, before the exam, perhaps make a list of words you struggle to spell but often find yourself using in essays, and commit them to memory.

The Globe Theatre's interior.

My (and Ashleigh's) hope is that this book, by demonstrating how to tease out themes from an extract, will help you feel more confident in doing so yourself. I believe it is also worth mentioning that the themes Ashleigh has picked out are by no means definitive. Asked the very same question, someone else may pick out different themes, and write an answer that is just as good (if not better!). Obviously the exam is not likely to be fun – my memory of them is pretty much the exact opposite. But still, this is one of the very few chances that you will get at GCSE level to actually be creative. And to my mind at least, that was always more enjoyable – if *enjoyable* is the right word – than simply demonstrating that I had memorised loads of facts.

At this point in the play, Prospero is opening up to Miranda about their family history for the first time.

PROSPERO

To have no screen between this part he play'd
And him he play'd it for, he needs will be
Absolute Milan. Me, poor man, my library
Was dukedom large enough: of temporal royalties
He thinks me now incapable; confederates--
So dry he was for sway--wi' the King of Naples
To give him annual tribute, do him homage,
Subject his coronet to his crown and bend
The dukedom yet unbow'd--alas, poor Milan!--
To most ignoble stooping.

MIRANDA

O the heavens!

PROSPERO

Mark his condition and the event; then tell me

If this might be a brother.
MIRANDA
I should sin
To think but nobly of my grandmother:
Good wombs have borne bad sons.

Starting with this moment in the play, explore how Shakespeare presents the concept of family.

Write about:

• How Shakespeare presents the concept of family at this moment in the play

• How Shakespeare presents the concept of family in the play as a whole.

Introduction

You want to keep the introduction fairly short and sweet, but also ensure it packs a punch – after all, you only have one chance to make a first impression on the examiner. I recommend starting the introduction with a short comment on historical context to score early AO3 marks. I would then suggest that you very quickly summarise the thematic gist of your essay.

"In Jacobean society, the institution of family was geared towards the perpetuation of male power: whereas the family patriarch was considered a head of state in miniature and the male heir his means of perpetuating power (hence Caliban's wish to have 'peopled' the isle 'with Calibans'), the wife was confined to the domestic, and younger women treated as bartering chips.[1] Yet while the overriding expectation on *any* individual was to treat family with deference and respect – an expectation Antonio is seen here to have violated – the idea that love and intimacy might also colour familial relationships does occasionally figure in the play."

Theme/Paragraph One: Shakespeare presents family as an institution which must be upheld, maintained, and treated with respect and reverence.

- Antonio's purported disrespect for Prospero as his elder and social better places his very position as brother in question: 'Mark his condition and the event; then tell me/ If this might be a brother.' Antonio's disrespect is cast here as at odds with his responsibilities to the familial institution, his betrayal undermining the honour of the family name. Tellingly, Shakespeare pushes the syllable count of the first of these two lines over the bounds of iambic pentameter, the metrical overstepping reflecting how Antonio's behaviour has overstepped a line.[2] [*AO1 for advancing the argument with a judiciously selected quote; AO2 for the close analysis of the language.*]
- That Antonio's machinations against his brother led the dukedom 'To most ignoble stooping' only redoubles the severity of his offence: not only has he

transgressed against the familial code of conduct, but the higher expectations placed on him as an aristocrat make the betrayal all the more acute.[3] The family's entire reputation has been compromised by Antonio's 'ignoble' conduct. To borrow the words of the treasonous brother in Shakespeare's *Hamlet* – Claudius – Antonio's 'offense is rank': not only foul, but all the more so given his 'rank.'[4] [*AO1 for advancing the argument with a judiciously selected quote; AO2 for the close analysis of the language.*]

- Elsewhere in the play: Sure enough, Antonio's disdain for family reappears in the play as he attempts to persuade Sebastian to kill King Alonso (Sebastian's brother) and seize the crown: 'Here lies your brother/No better than the earth he lies upon.' [*AO1 for advancing the argument with a judiciously selected quote.*]

- If Antonio eschews familial duty, Miranda on the other hand is presented here as the model of deference towards family and its hierarchies: she expresses an immediate and unquestioning respect for her grandmother — 'I should sin/ To think but nobly of my grandmother'— a woman she has never met but whom to think poorly of would be a 'sin.'[5] Crucially, it is the familial position of the grandmother as arch matriarch, and the broader institution of the noble family to which she belongs, that is important – not necessarily the woman herself.[6] [*AO1 for advancing the argument with a judiciously selected quote; AO2 for the close analysis of the language.*]

Theme/Paragraph Two: Family is presented as prioritising and centring around men.

- If Miranda – through the imbalance in the quantity of the dialogue, and her obliging tone – is presented as subservient to her father in this extract, this dynamic only intensifies as the play progresses.[7] Not only is Miranda expected to listen, 'hark' and 'mark' his words, and do his bidding ('pluck my magic garment from me'), but Prospero also frequently physically overpowers her with magic, causing her to fall asleep when she is not of use to him: 'Thou art inclined to sleep; 'tis a good dullness, /...I know thou canst not choose'. This is an extreme and supernatural example, but encapsulates the relative powerlessness of women in contemporaneous familial structures. [*AO1 for advancing the argument with a judiciously selected quote; AO2 for the close analysis of the language.*]

- This attitude towards women pervaded Jacobean England: a realm in which women did not have the right to own property, and where, upon their husbands' deaths, titles, land and wealth would pass either from father to son or from brother to brother. The play's very plot – which involves a brother's betrayal and attempted murder of his family – is emblematic of a patriarchal familial system, whereby the power and assets would automatically flow to the next male member of the family. [*AO3 for invoking relevant historical context.*]

- Elsewhere in the play: Act 5 marks a shift in political power in Prospero's favour: the reassignment of his dukedom restores his old power and his family's honour, while Miranda's marriage to Ferdinand betters it – as Gonzalo puts it: 'Was Milan thrust from Milan, that his issue/ Should become kings of Naples'. It is undoubtedly interesting that the marriage functions to transcend the boundaries between families (Ferdinand describes Prospero as 'a second father' and Alonso describes himself as the same to Miranda: 'I am hers'). Yet more interesting still is surely the primacy of the interests of the men at the heart of this union of families. Miranda transitions from daughter (an asset of her father) to wife (keeper of Ferdinand's house and bearer of children), while, in the process, enhancing her father's standing. [*AO1 for advancing the argument with a judiciously selected quote; AO2 for the close analysis of the language.*]

Theme/Paragraph Three: While family primarily figures as a patriarchal institution that places a variety of demands upon its members, there are times when it is also presented as a site of intimacy and affection.

- Just prior to this extract, the audience hears Prospero exclaim the extent to which he had loved his brother (and Miranda): 'he, whom next thyself / Of all the world I loved.' Although Prospero is asserting that he ranked Miranda and Antonio above anyone else in the world, the ambiguous formulation – 'of all the world' – leaves open the possibility that he loved them as much as existence ('the world') itself. While Antonio has since fallen out of favour, the implication is that not only was the fraternal affection intense, but Prospero still possesses considerable paternal affection for his daughter.[8] [*AO1 for advancing the argument with a judiciously selected quote; AO2 for the close analysis of the language.*]

- Even if one takes this rhetoric with a pinch of salt, this extract certainly shows a degree of intimacy between father and daughter: not only is Prospero clearly feeling an urge to confide in his daughter, but he is also looking for affirmation. Indeed, Prospero's probing words – 'tell me / If this might be a brother' – have the tenor of a question seeking an answer. Moreover, Prospero's anxiety that Miranda should take heed just prior to this extract – 'Dost thou attend me?'; 'Dost thou hear?' – arguably indicates not just his desire to control her, but a genuine hunger to receive emotional counsel. [*AO1 for advancing the argument with a judiciously selected quote; AO2 for the close analysis of the language.*]

- Elsewhere in the play: That Prospero later forces Ferdinand to carry logs – a gruelling pursuit that echoes Caliban's labours – to ensure he does not take Miranda for granted ('make the prize light'), could certainly be interpreted as another indication of the degree to which Prospero cherishes his daughter. [*AO1 for advancing the argument with a judiciously selected quote.*]

Theme / Paragraph Four: The play raises questions as to whether family must necessarily encompass only those related by genetic ties.

- Prospero here instructs Miranda to assess Antonio's conduct before deciding whether he ought to be considered a member of the family: 'Mark his condition and the event.' However, this question – whether a genetic relation might be disqualified from the family – implicitly invites another: whether a nongenetic relation could figure as a family member. [*AO1 for advancing the argument with a judiciously selected quote; AO2 for the close analysis of the language.*]

- In Act 5, Prospero sombrely states his relation to Caliban: 'This thing of darkness I / acknowledge mine.' Although this might most obviously point to the master/slave dynamic, other meanings lurk beneath the surface: perhaps Prospero is acknowledging himself as a surrogate father to Caliban; perhaps he is even acknowledging that the 'darkness' in Caliban is something he himself has instilled, as a father might hand down certain qualities to a son.[9] Moreover, the symmetries between Prospero and Caliban's true mother Sycorax – both are practitioners of magic; both keep Ariel as servant – bolster a sense of Prospero as a surrogate father to Caliban. [*AO1 for advancing the argument with a judiciously selected quote; AO2 for the close analysis of the language.*]

- If this argument is given credence, Caliban's attempted rape of Miranda takes on a Freudian dimension – it becomes a kind of attempt at incest – and Prospero's opprobrium arguably reveals contemporary anxieties about overlap between family and sexuality; anxieties which are articulated more explicitly still in such texts as John Ford's *Tis Pity She's a Whore*.[10] [*AO3 for invoking relevant literary-historical context.*]

Conclusion

This is a meaty essay, and I've covered all the major themes I was hoping to hit. However, because I still want the conclusion to keep the examiner's attention, I've decided to bring in a character I haven't yet acknowledged – Claribel – as a mechanism to tie up loose ends with a bit of panache.

"Sebastian notes that Claribel (Alonso's daughter) 'Weigh'd between loathness and obedience' when undertaking her marriage to the 'King of Tunis': the wedding from which Alonso and his company are retuning at the play's inception. Indeed, Claribel's experiences neatly encapsulate many of the ways the play conceives of family: not only are her choices dictated by familial duty (she was 'obedient' to her father's will), but the dynamic ultimately advances the needs and desires of men. After all, while it may have induced 'loathness' in Claribel, she nevertheless went ahead with a marriage designed entirely to bolster her father's power."

An illustration from the artist Robert Anning Bell, depicting the immediate aftermath of the storm in the opening scene.

A t this point in the play, Ariel has reminded Prospero about his promise to free him.

PROSPERO

[...] it was mine art,
When I arrived and heard thee, that made gape
The pine and let thee out.

ARIEL

I thank thee, master.

PROSPERO

If thou more murmur'st, I will rend an oak
And peg thee in his knotty entrails till
Thou hast howl'd away twelve winters.

ARIEL

Pardon, master;
I will be correspondent to command
And do my spiriting gently.

PROSPERO

Do so, and after two days

I will discharge thee.
ARIEL
That's my noble master!
What shall I do? say what; what shall I do?

Starting with this moment in the play, explore how far Shakespeare presents Prospero as a kind master.

Write about:

• How Shakespeare presents Prospero at this moment in the play.

• How Shakespeare presents Prospero's treatment of his servants in the play as a whole.

Introduction

Again, I am kicking things off with a nod to the wider context of the play and its performance history. This will score you early AO3 marks and lay a foundation of understanding within which your later AO1 insights can be contextualised. It can also be useful to define your understanding of the question's key terms: in this case 'kind' and 'master,' and to hint at the characters that will be at the heart of your essay.

"*The Tempest* is one of Shakespeare's later plays, estimated to have been written between 1610 and 1611 and first performed by the King's Men in the

court of King James I. At this point in history, Britain
was nearing its peak in the trade of enslaved peoples
abducted from colonised lands, so the use of 'master'
to describe Prospero comes with considerable
historical baggage. If we are to see Ariel and Caliban
as the equivalents of enslaved natives, this will
necessarily complicate our perception of behaviour
that might be construed as kind – a concept bound up
with ideas of generosity, consideration, and mild self-
sacrifice."

**Theme/Paragraph One: The portrait painted of
Prospero by his underlings offers a complicated
picture: whereas Ariel is equivocal, Caliban is
damning.** [1]

- In this extract, Ariel greets Prospero as 'my noble
  master'. The word 'noble' encompasses ideas of moral
  superiority, goodness and virtue. It also suggests that
  Ariel conceives of Prospero as being of 'noble' birth: a
  member of the aristocracy, a rank which at the time
  would have been automatically seen as worthy of
  respect, especially given that this play was first
  performed in court in front of an audience of noble-
  born aristocrats. In fact, many of the appellations
  Ariel bestows upon Prospero are evocative of respect
  and awe, but not necessarily kindness. He addresses
  Prospero variously as 'sir', 'my lord' and 'master', each
  suggesting Prospero's virtue and fitness to rule over
  him, as well as describing him as 'great' in his first line
  of Act 2 Scene 2 – 'all hail great master' – which is
  once again a word associated with power and nobility.

Notably, while Shakespeare might as easily have used the word 'good' – a word with stronger semantic ties to kindness – he opted instead for 'great': a word that more readily conjures notions of power. [*AO1 for advancing the argument with a judiciously selected quote; AO2 for the close analysis of the language; AO3 for invoking relevant historical context.*]

- Whereas Ariel's depiction of Prospero is somewhat equivocal, Caliban's portrayal of Prospero is not. As Caliban bluntly puts it: 'I am subject to a tyrant, a/ sorcerer, that by his cunning hath cheated me of the island.' While Ariel seems willing and eager to perform his master's will – 'What shall I do? say what; what shall I do?' – Caliban strongly resents his position of servitude ('I must obey'). Judging by their own assessments, then, one might infer that Prospero is a kinder master to Ariel than he is to Caliban. [*AO1 for advancing the argument with a judiciously selected quote; AO2 for the close analysis of the language.*]

Theme/Paragraph Two: Caliban arguably has every right to hate Prospero to such a degree: Prospero frequently abuses *both* of his servants physically and verbally

- In Act 1 Scene 2 Prospero describes Caliban as 'A freckled whelp hag-born--not honour'd with/ A human shape'; and after Caliban curses Prospero—'a south-west blow on ye/ And blister you all o'er!'— Prospero suppresses his servant's outrage with the visceral threat of 'cramps' and 'Side-stitches'. There are echoes here of Antony's cruel abuse of power – 'Take hence this Jack, and whip him' – in *Antony and*

Cleopatra, another of Shakespeare's later plays. [*AO1 for advancing the argument with a judiciously selected quote; AO2 for the close analysis of the language; AO3 for invoking relevant historical context.*]

- Equally, in the extract above, Prospero also threatens Ariel: 'I will rend an oak/ And peg thee in his knotty entrails till/Thou hast howl'd away twelve winters.' Not only are Prospero's threats detailed and verbose – the sentence enjambs over multiple lines, the syntax knotting the listener – but it also cruelly exploits Ariel's profoundly personal fears of being re-imprisoned in the pine tree from which Prospero freed him.[2] Prospero's threat of 'peg[ging]' Ariel up in an oak tree, rather than another pine, suggests that Prospero's wrath is even greater than that of the evil witch Sycorax and his punishments harsher, since oak is a stronger, knottier wood. Prospero's ability to use his powers to punish his servants for disobeying, or even simply displeasing him slightly, would strongly suggest that Shakespeare does not present Prospero as a kind master, either in the above quote or elsewhere in the play. [*AO1 for advancing the argument with a judiciously selected quote; AO2 for the close analysis of the language and for discussing how form shapes meaning.*]

- Perhaps Ariel's eagerness to serve and please Prospero – 'I come/To answer thy best pleasure' – is a product of fear rather than respect. The appellations discussed above sustain this notion: by addressing Prospero as 'sir', 'lord', 'noble' and 'great', Ariel is more likely respecting his master's power, *not* paying tribute to his kindness. [*AO1 for advancing the argument with a judiciously selected quote; AO2 for the close analysis of the language.*]

Theme/Paragraph Three: Shakespeare does not present Prospero as entirely unkind, but his kindness is entirely conditional.

- Many interactions between Prospero and Ariel are extremely affectionate: in the play's final scene, he addresses Ariel as 'My Ariel, chick', and elsewhere as 'fine spirit' and 'my brave spirit', all suggesting a sense of almost paternal pride in his servant.[3] He even goes as far as to say he loves him 'dearly'. [*AO1 for advancing the argument with a judiciously selected quote; AO2 for the close analysis of the language.*]

- However, Prospero's kindness is conditional. Prospero, in the extract above, makes clear that he will only grant Ariel his freedom should he follow Prospero's orders ('Do so, and.../ I will discharge thee'); and, sure enough, the words of affection already cited come only once Ariel has completed Prospero's bidding. Conversely, the merest murmur of dissent from Ariel is enough to elicit Prospero's wrath. The way Prospero blows hot and cold with Ariel is encoded into the nuances of his language. A case in point is Prospero's use of 'thou', an informal pronoun that he uses by turns both affectionately and derogatively. When Prospero uses 'thou' in the extract above – 'If thou more murmur'st' – he is asserting dominance, whereas when he speaks in praise of Ariel – 'Bravely, my diligence. Thou shalt be free' – his use is affectionate and intimate. The usage is a microcosm of Prospero's power. [*AO1 for advancing the argument with a judiciously selected quote; AO2 for close language analysis.*]

- Although by the time the audience encounters Caliban he is firmly in Prospero's bad books, it is clear that he had also once upon a time enjoyed Prospero's kindness on a conditional basis. Prospero had once 'strokedst' and 'madest much of' him – that is, until Caliban forsook this treatment with his attempted rape of Miranda: 'thou didst seek to violate/The honour of my child.' [*AO1 for advancing the argument with a judiciously selected quote.*]

Theme/Paragraph Four: Prospero might also be considered Miranda's master, though his relationship with her again defies easy categorisation: what some may interpret as kind and protective, others might consider domineering.

- While not in the servile position Ariel and Caliban find themselves in, Miranda is also in Prospero's thrall: he uses his power to put her to sleep – 'thou art inclined to sleep ... / give it way' – and to stage-manage an elaborate rendezvous with Ferdinand that is intended to coerce her into developing feelings for him.[4] That Miranda believes she is rebelling against her father in pursuing Ferdinand, even as she is in fact doing exactly what Prospero had intended, only underscores the degree of his mastery over her. [*AO1 for advancing the argument with a judiciously selected quote.*]
- In Jacobean times, it was quite normal for aristocratic fathers to be involved in their daughter's marriage,

since their own power and prestige was at stake: in fact, by the standards of the time, Prospero's concern for Miranda's wellbeing – as illustrated by such comments as 'I have done nothing but in care of thee' – would have been considered above and beyond. Yet a modern audience may hear the overly domineering attitude of 'I will discharge thee' – the words Prospero addresses to Ariel in this extract – in his realpolitik approach to marrying Miranda off to Ferdinand, and might ponder what consequences Miranda would have faced had she not gelled with Ferdinand so readily.[5] [*AO1 for advancing the argument with a judiciously selected quote; AO2 for close language analysis.*]

Conclusion

Again, I feel confident that the essay is covering all of my bases. Although much of the conclusion is a recap, I have striven to finish it off with a new observation that demonstrates to the examiner that I'm still probing the essay's central question.

_____

"While by modern standards Prospero would most likely be construed as abusive and changeable – all the more so given Caliban has increasingly been portrayed as a sympathetic character in modern productions – the generosity and praise he extends to Ariel (*and* Caliban at the start of their relationship) would have exceeded what was expected in a master/ 'slave' dynamic. Indeed, it should not be overlooked that Prospero at the end of the play frees not only Ariel, whom he had promised to liberate, but also Caliban. Yet if this is arguably Prospero's single act of pure kindness, it is important to note that it necessarily coincides with Prospero abdicating his role of master."[6]

An illustration of Sycorax — again from the artist Robert Anning Bell.

A t this point in the play Prospero is visiting
Caliban to give him orders.

PROSPERO
Abhorred slave,
Which any print of goodness wilt not take,
Being capable of all ill! I pitied thee,
Took pains to make thee speak, taught thee each hour
One thing or other: when thou didst not, savage,
Know thine own meaning, but wouldst gabble like
A thing most brutish, I endow'd thy purposes
With words that made them known. But thy vile race,
Though thou didst learn, had that in't which good
        natures
Could not abide to be with; therefore wast thou
Deservedly confined into this rock,
Who hadst deserved more than a prison.
CALIBAN
You taught me language; and my profit on't
Is, I know how to curse. The red plague rid you

For learning me your language!

Starting with this moment in the play, explore how Shakespeare presents the importance of education.

Write about:

• How Shakespeare presents the importance of education at this moment in the play.

• How Shakespeare presents the importance of education in the play as a whole.

Introduction

Sometimes it is useful to dive straight into analysis in your introduction. This can be done by means of a handle or a hook from which you can hang the rest of your themes: here, for example, we might use the hook 'knowledge is power' and see how that relates to the representation of education in the play. However, even though I've decided to mix things up slightly, notice that I am still striving to score early AO3 marks – this time by citing a text that Shakespeare would have been familiar with, and which *The Tempest* seems to echo.

"In an artful literalisation of the adage that 'knowledge is power', Prospero's books – the symbols of his knowledge and education – function as the source of his 'potent art', his magic.[1] The use of 'art' as a synonym for magic equates the humanitarian studies with a kind of supernatural power that grants Prospero the ability to govern the island and control the elements, and, in so doing, echoes precursory texts such as Chaucer's *The Franklin's Tale*, in which a scholar-cum-magician similarly draws magical powers from his scholarly pursuits.[2] Shakespeare in this extract explores the intersection between education and power, while also probing broader colonial attitudes towards education."

Theme/Paragraph One: Education is presented as a means of betterment and refinement.

- In this extract, Prospero describes how he refined Caliban through education: whereas Caliban previously 'wouldst gabble like / A thing most brutish,' Prospero – by taking 'pains to make [Caliban] speak' and teaching him 'each hour / One thing or another' – brought Caliban to coherency and fluency. Fittingly, in this speech about the benefits of education and language, Prospero makes use of a number of rhetorical devices. In the line 'Took pains to make thee speak, taught thee each hour' alone, not only is there structural parallelism around the caesura with the repetition of 'thee' and the consonance of 'took' and 'taught', but also an effective use of stark monosyllabism – a technique which artfully telegraphs Prospero's shortness of temper, while also achieving clarity with its simplicity.[3] [*AO1 for advancing the argument with a judiciously selected quote; AO2 for the close analysis of the language and for discussing how form shapes meaning.*]

- Later in the speech, Prospero's language flowers into polysyllabic clusters and phonetical arrangements that challenge the tongue; in the line 'therefore wast thou/ Deservedly confined', the transition between the consonant cluster of 'st' to the 'th' sound in 'thou,' is a difficult one, and requires a high level of lingual agility.[4] The structural transition between simple semantics to complex structures perhaps mirrors the process of Caliban being educated from baseness to eloquence. [*AO1 for advancing the argument with a judiciously selected quote; AO2 for the close analysis of the language.*]

- Sure enough, Caliban too speaks with incredible eloquence: like Prospero, he communicates in verse, and he makes use of devices such as consonance ('learning me your language').[5] However, while it has the potential to refine, education is depicted as bettering only insofar as the person being educated is willing to use it in a good or appropriate way, and Prospero is appalled that Caliban uses language instead to express his carnal lust for Miranda and ill-will towards his master, as he does here: 'my profit on't / Is, I know how to curse.' Indeed, Prospero presents education as being appropriate only for a certain kind of person, contending that Caliban's 'vile race [...] Could not abide to be with' the 'good' that education brings. This colonial sentiment would have tallied with broader Jacobean sentiments in an era that saw colonisers often imposing Westernised education on foreign peoples, while also maintaining the racist belief that these native peoples were on some fundamental level less advanced than the European invaders, regardless of education. [*AO1 for advancing the argument with a judiciously selected quote; AO2 for the close analysis of the language; AO3 for invoking relevant historical context.*]

Theme/Paragraph Two: Although Prospero figures as an educator in a number of ways, he tends to conceive of education as valuable only insofar as it enhances his power.

- Prospero's plan regarding the shipwrecked aristocrats can also be seen as an education of sorts. Alonzo, Sebastian, and Antonio must be made to take ownership of their crimes against Prospero, and reinstate him as Duke of Milan; Miranda must learn of her family history and how to interact with nobles as a noble herself; and Ariel must learn the price of freedom. However, there is a common thread here: imparting these lessons directly bolsters Prospero's position and standing. As far as Prospero is concerned, education is valuable only insofar as it enhances his position. [*AO1 for advancing the argument.*]

- Arguably, Prospero's disgust towards Caliban in this extract is the result also of the fact that educating Caliban has not enhanced Prospero's power to the degree he had hoped. Indeed, if it had in fact been power (as opposed to pity) that had motivated Prospero in the first place, Prospero's claim in this extract – 'I pitied thee' – seems like an attempt at spin; as though Prospero is rewriting history to grant himself a sheen of virtuosity. However, while

Prospero might deem Caliban a failed project, the very fact he has induced Caliban to internalise his language is still a power exchange – one in which Prospero has displaced Caliban's native tongue, and implicitly forced Caliban to pay homage to a European culture. [*AO1 for advancing the argument with a judiciously selected quote; AO2 for the close analysis of the language.*]

- In contrast to Prospero, the Caliban that Prospero and Miranda first encountered on the island was a far purer form of educator: Caliban 'show'd [Prospero] all the qualities o' the isle' and taught him about the geography and natural workings of its assets, while not expecting anything in return. Ironically, however, one of the key lessons Caliban has since learnt from Prospero is only to impart knowledge when it stands to enhance your power – hence Caliban's evident regret for the hospitality he showed: 'the red plague rid you.' [*AO1 for advancing the argument with a judiciously selected quote.*]

Theme/Paragraph Three: While Shakespeare, through Prospero, presents education as an important means of reconciling power, he also paradoxically uses Prospero to demonstrate how education can distract with disastrous consequences for one's standing.[6]

- Although this extract appears just as Prospero – after a colossal wait, and a stroke of luck – has finally managed to ensnare the countrymen who betrayed him, Prospero here seems instead utterly distracted with the topic of education. This hints at another dimension to education: while it facilitates Prospero's power, it also figures as a distraction that paradoxically threatens to undercut his power altogether. [*AO2 for discussing how structure shapes meaning.*]

- Elsewhere in the play, this dynamic is most vividly captured in Prospero's original fall from grace in Milan. Prospero – as he explains to Miranda when detailing how they wound up on the island – describes how his neglecting of 'worldly ends' in the pursuit of 'the bettering of [his] mind' led to his brother seizing power and attempting to murder him: his library may have been 'dukedom large enough', but it was not the only dukedom he should have been governing. Here Shakespeare presents education as an integral catalyst for the drama of *The Tempest*, but also as an endeavour that has the potential to distract people from more important aspects of life, such as family and social duties.[7] [*AO1 for advancing the argument with a judiciously selected quote; AO2 for the close analysis of the language.*]

- At the end of the play, Prospero 'drown[s]' his books in order to devote himself more fully to the material world and the duties of his reinstated dukedom. Though his 'art' was derived from education and facilitated the control of the island and the re-education of the shipwrecked nobles, there are certain practical engagements such as governing for which presence and experience are perhaps more useful than education. Shakespeare, then, while portraying education as an important ingredient in the brokerage of power, seems to caution the need for moderation in pursuing it. [*AO1 for advancing the argument with a judiciously selected quote language.*]

Conclusion

On this occasion, I feel as though my essay has been a little bit lacking on the AO3 front. As a result, I have baked literary context into the conclusion to ensure I am still picking up those marks.

"While the cerebral, university-educated protagonist of Shakespeare's eponymous play *Hamlet* demonstrates tremendous powers of eloquence, when it comes to taking action, Hamlet's education functions to distract: his hand-wringing 'to be or not to be' induces stasis.[8] Yet while – as Hamlet and Prospero both demonstrate – education can be a fatal distraction, it is still an essential ingredient for any would-be ruler. Certainly, it is telling that Caliban asserts that Prospero would be a 'sot' without his books: a word that has connotations of idiocy and drunkenness. The subtext is plain: without education, one risks winding up like Trinculo: immoral, venal, base and corrupt."

An interpretation of *The Tempest* from the artist William Hogarth.

At this point in the play, Antonio is trying to convince Sebastian to kill his brother.

ANTONIO
Nor I; my spirits are nimble.
They fell together all, as by consent;
They dropp'd, as by a thunder-stroke. What might,
Worthy Sebastian? O, what might?--No more:--
And yet me thinks I see it in thy face,
What thou shouldst be: the occasion speaks thee, and
My strong imagination sees a crown
Dropping upon thy head.
SEBASTIAN
What, art thou waking?
ANTONIO
Do you not hear me speak?
SEBASTIAN
I do; and surely
It is a sleepy language and thou speak'st

Out of thy sleep. What is it thou didst say?
This is a strange repose, to be asleep
With eyes wide open; standing, speaking, moving,
And yet so fast asleep.
ANTONIO
Noble Sebastian,
Thou let'st thy fortune sleep--die, rather; wink'st
Whiles thou art waking.

Starting with this moment in the play, explore how Shakespeare presents the relationship between sleep and power.

Write about:

• How Shakespeare presents sleep at this moment in the play.

• How Shakespeare presents the relationship between sleep and power in the play as a whole.

Introduction

Unlike some of the other questions in this guide, here the examiner is asking you to look at two things in relation to one another – sleep and power – as opposed to just one idea in isolation. This form of question is undoubtedly harder, and it is important to try and acknowledge both "strands" of the question in the introduction.

On this occasion, I have invoked a quote from a different sixteenth century poet that deals with the intersection between sleep and power and have used that as a springboard.

"Whereas Sir Philip Sidney conceived of sleep as a powerful leveller – his late sixteenth century poem, 'Sleep,' dubbed it 'the indifferent judge between high and low' – sleep in *The Tempest* figures as a more complicated phenomenon. For although on one hand it *is* presented as a leveller – Prospero assures Miranda that Ferdinand is human by observing he 'eats and sleeps' – it also figures as something that might be induced in others, or exploited (in the way, for instance, Sebastian and Antonio plot to exploit Alonso's sudden descent into sleep in this extract), in order to gain an upper hand."

Theme/Paragraph One: When characters are asleep, they are vulnerable. Here Alonso is in danger of being murdered by his brother as he is unable to protect himself. Caliban, Stephano and Trinculo plot to kill Prospero in his sleep later in the play.

- In this extract, Alonso and Gonzalo are sleeping, having been charmed by Ariel. Sebastian and Antonio therefore have power over them – their 'spirits' remain 'nimble' – and could seemingly kill them without meeting any resistance. Socially speaking, Alonso, the

King of Naples, is both Antonio and Sebastian's better and has more power than them both; yet, since he is asleep, he is vulnerable to his powers being seized and displaced to his brother via his death. With Alonso asleep and his power suspended, Antonio becomes the most powerful person in the scene, using the power of persuasion to convince Sebastian to usurp his brother.[1] Indeed, the idea of sleep representing an opportunity to redistribute power is a recurring one in Shakespeare, this plot echoing Macbeth and Lady Macbeth's violent seizure of power through the murder of a slumbering King – the 'unguarded Duncan' – in *Macbeth*. [*AO1 for advancing the argument with a judiciously selected quote; AO3 for invoking relevant literary context.*]

- Sleep is also presented as a state of powerlessness elsewhere in the play: when Caliban, for instance, suggests that Stephano and Trinculo kill Prospero: 'tis a custom with him,/ I' th' afternoon to sleep: there thou mayst brain him'. Ironically, were this plan to have succeeded, Prospero's power to put people to sleep would have been removed as a result of him having been asleep himself. In the final scene, Boatswain asserts that he and the rest of the crew 'were dead of sleep': that is to say, while they had been asleep, they had been as powerless as if they had been dead. [*AO1 for advancing the argument with a judiciously selected quote; AO2 for the close analysis of the language.*]

Theme/Paragraph Two: Sleep is used as a metaphor for inaction or dormancy: to be awake and to fail to exert one's power is to engage in a kind of metaphorical sleep.

- It is notable that Antonio accuses Sebastian of letting his 'fortune sleep--die, rather', meaning that he is letting a good opportunity pass him by. Here 'fortune' and the sleeping Alonso are conflated: if Sebastian allows both Alonso and fortune to sleep, he will be killing his opportunity – instead, in order to take the opportunity, Sebastian must kill Alonso. Shakespeare's use of anacoluthon in Antontio's line clarifies his point with a sense of finality: if this opportunity is missed, it will not come around again, it will 'die'.[2] Thus Antonio frames the decision *not* to kill Alonso – that is, *not* to induce a kind of permanent sleep – as an instance of metaphorical sleep and weakness. [*AO1 for advancing the argument with a judiciously selected quote; AO2 for the close analysis of the language.*]

Theme/Paragraph Three: While Sebastian and Alonso appear to have the power over the sleepers, the very fact that their countrymen are asleep reminds the audience of the true power broker, Prospero, and his transcendent ability to induce sleep in the first place.

- Antonio's description of how the rest of their coterie fell asleep is striking: he observes that they dropped with uncanny synchronicity – 'fell together all' – and as if 'by a thunder-stroke.' The power to induce sleep is thus given an air of almost Zeus-like transcendence: Prospero – via Ariel – is the thunderer who brought about this circumstance; a pseudo-deity smiting individuals with sleep.[3] That Prospero later neuters Sebastian and Antonio with the threat of revealing their attempt to kill Alonso – 'at this time/ I will tell no tales' – indicates that, even though Sebastian and Antonio *seem* to have the power in this sequence, really it had been a trap all along. Indeed, their power had been illusory, as Ariel had been overseeing events on Prospero's behalf. [*AO1 for advancing the argument with a judiciously selected quote; AO2 for the close analysis of the language.*]

- If this sequence reminds the audience of Prospero's transcendent capacity to induce sleep, it is notable that, in the play's final scene, we are told also of Prospero's power to raise the dead – a power perhaps more awesome than any other – and this is tellingly framed as a kind of reversal of his powers of sleep induction: 'graves at my command/Have waked their sleepers.' [*AO1 for advancing the argument with a judiciously selected quote; AO2 for the close analysis of the language.*]

Theme/Paragraph Four: The ability to introduce dream-like phenomena into reality – in other words, phenomena that is intimately related to sleep – is a key means of brokering power in *The Tempest*.

- As a result of their ability to control when and the degree to which dream-like phenomena are allowed to intrude on reality – be it supernatural visitations, such as Ariel appearing before the king's party and declaring 'I have made you mad, or the eerie music –

Prospero and Ariel are invested with the potent power to induce uncertainty in others about reality. [*AO1 for advancing the argument with a judiciously selected quote.*]

- Yet while this power resides chiefly with Prospero and Ariel, it is occasionally wielded by others. Here, Antonio, through language alone, conjures a potent vision of Sebastian being crowned with his brother's crown – 'My strong imagination sees a crown/ Dropping upon thy head' – and Sebastian seems to construe this image as the stuff of dreams ('thou speak's/ Out of thy sleep') – presumably because such ambitions occupy Sebastian's dreams. Sure enough, the introduction of this dream-like vision induces confusion in Sebastian, as he becomes uncertain of whether he is asleep or awake – he talks of being 'asleep/ With eyes wide open', the enjambment over the line break mirroring the blurred line between sleep and waking – and this makes him pliable to Antonio's demands. [*AO1 for advancing the argument with a judiciously selected quote; AO2 for the close analysis of the language.*]

Conclusion

"Many critics have linked Prospero's power to Shakespeare's power as the writer. Prospero sends whole parties to sleep to keep them dormant until the time is right to deal with them just as Shakespeare opts to use different characters in different scenes. Moreover, Prospero creates fictional, dream-like visions – be it the storm at the start that was not truly a bona-

fide storm, or the masque – in much the same way as
Shakespeare conjures the entire fictional world the
dramatis personae inhabit.[4] The real power, then, lies
with Shakespeare, whose play itself is a kind of an
extended dream, and whose characters 'are such stuff /
As dreams are made on.'"

Another illustration from Robert Anning
Bell — this time depicting Ariel waking
Gonzalo just before Antonio and
Sebastian can carry out their regicidal
ambitions.

Trinculo and Stephano encounter Caliban for the first time.

TRINCULO

I shall laugh myself to death at this puppy-headed monster. A most scurvy monster! I could find in my heart to beat him,--

STEPHANO

Come, kiss.

TRINCULO

But that the poor monster's in drink: an abominable monster!

CALIBAN

I'll show thee the best springs; I'll pluck thee berries;
I'll fish for thee and get thee wood enough.
A plague upon the tyrant that I serve!
I'll bear him no more sticks, but follow thee,
Thou wondrous man.

TRINCULO

A most ridiculous monster, to make a wonder of a
Poor drunkard!

CALIBAN

I prithee, let me bring thee where crabs grow;
And I with my long nails will dig thee pignuts;
Show thee a jay's nest and instruct thee how
To snare the nimble marmoset; I'll bring thee
To clustering filberts and sometimes I'll get thee
Young scamels from the rock. Wilt thou go with me?

Starting with this moment in the play, explore how Shakespeare presents Caliban as monstrous

Write about:

• How Shakespeare presents Caliban at this moment in the play.

• How Shakespeare presents Caliban in the play as a whole.

Introduction

With a question like this, it is always worth interrogating the key terms: what does 'monstrous' mean to you? What might the word 'monster' mean in the context of the extract? By pulling apart the word, it is possible to access a greater breadth of analysis. As ever, though, notice how I have slotted context (AO3-scoring material) into the introduction.

"The word 'monstrous' typically suggests something large, frightening, bestial and of malicious intent. Many of these traits can be seen to apply to Caliban up to a point: while kind to some, he is of malicious intent towards Prospero (and arguably also Miranda), and his appearance frequently shocks. Yet given that *The Tempest* is a product of a time in which the trade of enslaved peoples was commonplace, it is perhaps fair to contend that Caliban is not intrinsically monstrous; rather, he is defined as such by a culture that wishes to justify his subjugation. Instead, Caliban might more readily fit a more subtle definition of 'monstrous': that is, something 'other'; something unrecognizable in form or behaviour."

Theme/Paragraph One: Caliban is articulate and subservient, and he bears neither Stephano or Trinculo any ill will. In fact, he is initially frightened that they may be Prospero's spirits come to torment him.

- The word monster arguably connotes a lack of humanity – be that in behaviour or appearance: monsters are often considered brutish and unintelligent. However, Caliban is extremely articulate, often more so than Trinculo and Stephano: for instance, he speaks in verse where Trinculo speaks in prose (or, alternatively, in such irregular verse that it might as well be prose). Shakespeare often uses prose to signify the lower status or baseness of ignoble characters. Although neither Trinculo or Stephano could be considered particularly noble, one might expect the supposed 'monster' in the scene to be depicted as baser and less articulate. [*AO2 for discussing how form shapes meaning.*]

- Caliban's language is laden with rich natural imagery and promises pertaining to it: 'I'll show thee the best springs; I'll pluck thee berries.' The anaphora here marks the beginning of a refrain of future tense transient verbs that continue to appear throughout, showing an almost over-zealous eagerness to please and serve.[1] Indeed, when Caliban's verse does occasionally overspill its ten syllables of iambic pentameter, it is when he is attempting to fit the word 'thee' into his lines: the form yields to reflect how Caliban sacrifices his regular structure to accommodate his new companions. This obsequiousness seems far from monstrous, especially if one is to equate wildness with monstrosity.[2] On the contrary, Caliban's command over language and his intention to serve and obey depict him as positively tamed and subjugated. [*AO1 for advancing the argument with a judiciously selected quote; AO2 for the close analysis of the language.*]

- Indeed, we are told earlier in the play that this is exactly what has happened: Prospero 'tamed' and educated Caliban – he 'Took pains to make [him] speak.' Perhaps, then, Shakespeare is suggesting that Caliban *had* been monstrous, yet the monstrosity had been exorcised from him as he had been taught to speak and serve. [*AO1 for advancing the argument with a judiciously selected quote.*]

Theme/Paragraph Two: Caliban's physical appearance may also be seen as monstrous by the standards of the time.

- If monstrosity is seen as synonymous with ugliness or a fearful appearance, then Caliban may indeed be considered monstrous: we are told he looks and smells like a 'strange fish', he has 'long nails', and Miranda admits that she does 'not like to look on' him. This is perhaps rooted in contemporaneous colonial racism: it was widely held at the time that monsters abounded in foreign lands, such as the 'blemmyes' who were believed to roam the deserts of Eastern Africa with no heads and faces on their torsos. Colonised peoples were considered in the same bracket as these fictional monsters in the popular imagination, and since Caliban was a native on the island before Prospero arrived, many scholars see parallels between Shakespeare's presentation of Caliban and contemporary racist views of indigenous populations of invaded countries. [*AO1 for advancing the argument with a judiciously selected quote; AO3 for invoking historically relevant context.*]

- Caliban's 'monstrous' otherness might therefore be seen as racial otherness constructed by Eurocentric ideals of the time. Indeed, none of the characters who describe Caliban as a monster are natives of the island themselves. [*AO3 for invoking historically relevant context.*]

- Although there is plenty to suggest that Caliban is aesthetically displeasing to the other characters, there are also very few specifics to pin him down, and some of the descriptors seem in fact to clash: Trinculo here calls him 'puppy-headed' in this extract and 'a strange fish' just beforehand; Stephano labels him a 'moon-calf'; and Prospero describes him as being of 'human-shape', but also calls him a 'whelp' and 'tortoise.' What is perhaps monstrous to the Europeans, then, is not just Caliban's "otherness", but also the way he seems to defy categorisation. [*AO1 for advancing the argument with a judiciously selected quote; AO2 for the close analysis of the language.*]

Theme/Paragraph Three: Although Caliban may look monstrous and he may have behaved monstrously in his attempted rape of Miranda and plotted murder of Prospero, are his actions really any more monstrous than those of the other characters in the play?

- In this extract, Trinculo describes Caliban as 'an abominable monster', abominable here meaning morally repellent. Trinculo uses this word as Caliban is drunk on the liquor they have given him, and persistent drunkenness was widely considered a morally base quality at the time. However, Trinculo and Stephano are themselves drunk and Alonso describes Stephano as his 'drunken butler', suggesting that this is more of a character trait than the transient state Caliban is exhibiting. How, then, can Caliban be seen as more abominable than his new companions? [*AO1 for advancing the argument with a judiciously selected quote; AO2 for the close analysis of the language.*]
- Indeed, Caliban's drunkenness is the only thing

stopping Trinculo from beating him: 'I could find in my/ heart to beat him,— [...] But that the poor monster's in drink'. The desire to beat the defenceless Caliban could itself be seen as monstrous. [*AO1 for advancing the argument with a judiciously selected quote.*]

- Certainly, monstrousness that is entirely unrelated to Caliban pervades the play: Antonio's usurpation of his brother and his attempt to persuade Sebastian to kill their king could be considered monstrous. Prospero, too, can be seen as monstrous in his treatment of his servants, especially Ariel whose pleas for freedom are met with threats of being [pegged] in an 'oak tree' for twelve years. However, none of these characters are described as monsters. It seems, then, that Caliban's monstrosity must be the result primarily of his "otherness" to the European characters – since his actions do not appear to be more monstrous than those of these other individuals. [*AO1 for advancing the argument with a judiciously selected quote; AO2 for the close analysis of the language.*]

Conclusion

"While the Jewish Shylock in Shakespeare's *The Merchant of Venice* is construed as monstrous by so many of the Christian contingent – he is labelled 'the very devil' by his servant, for instance – Shylock is not alone in engaging in what might be deemed monstrous behaviour; in fact, in many ways he merely repays the persecution he receives. Likewise, Caliban – a 'born devil', as Prospero dubs him – is a kind of ethnic "other" who is characterised as monstrous by those who often treat him monstrously. When, in the final scene, Prospero takes ownership of Caliban – 'This thing of darkness I/ acknowledge mine' – it is hard not to hear him take ownership of Caliban's monstrosity, too: Caliban is a 'thing of darkness' because Prospero made him so."

Johann Heinrich Ramberg's depiction of Shakespeare's Caliban (far left) dancing with Stephano and Tinculo.

At this point in the play, Miranda and Ferdinand find themselves alone for the first time.

FERDINAND
[...] Full many a lady
I have eyed with best regard and many a time
The harmony of their tongues hath into bondage
Brought my too diligent ear: for several virtues
Have I liked several women; never any
With so full soul, but some defect in her
Did quarrel with the noblest grace she owed
And put it to the foil: but you, O you,
So perfect and so peerless, are created
Of every creature's best!
MIRANDA
I do not know
One of my sex; no woman's face remember,
Save, from my glass, mine own; nor have I seen

More that I may call men than you, good friend,
And my dear father: how features are abroad,
I am skilless of; but, by my modesty,
The jewel in my dower, I would not wish
Any companion in the world but you,
Nor can imagination form a shape,
Besides yourself, to like of.

Starting with this moment in the play, explore how Shakespeare presents romantic attraction.

Write about:

• **How Shakespeare presents romantic attraction at this moment in the play.**

• **How Shakespeare presents romantic attraction in the play as a whole.**

Introduction

"In Shakespeare's England, romantic attraction in the aristocratic classes (such as those both Miranda and Ferdinand belong to) was expressed and acted upon through rituals of courtship. In fact, the word courtship directly relates to the conduct of suitors towards ladies in court while attempting to woo them. Courtship in the Elizabethan and Jacobean aristocracy took the form of gift-giving, acts of favour, witty and flirtatious conversation and compliments.

Many of these acts of courtship can be seen in Shakespeare's presentation of Miranda and Ferdinand's romantic attraction, and would have been intimately familiar to the play's initial royal and courtly audience in 1611."

Theme/Paragraph One: This is the first time Miranda has been romantically attracted to anyone, and, from her perspective, romantic attraction is portrayed as new and exciting. From Ferdinand's perspective the level of romantic attraction is presented as new, though he has been attracted to other women before.

- Since the age of three, Miranda has encountered no man other than her father and the spirits that inhabit the island: 'This/ Is the third man that e'er I saw, the first/ That e'er I sigh'd for'. Shakespeare's use of parallel syntax here directly aligns the act of 'seeing' with the act of 'sighing', and further solidifies their bond with sibilance, suggesting that romantic attraction was largely motivated by sight – or, rather, her admiration of Ferdinand's physical appearance. In fact, when Ferdinand first appears before her, she assumes him to be a 'spirit' or a 'thing divine' bearing a 'brave form'. Ferdinand assumes a similar thing of Miranda, describing her immediately as a 'goddess' and a 'wonder'. [*AO1 for advancing the argument with a judiciously selected quote; AO2 for the close analysis of the language.*]
- The difference here is that Ferdinand – by his own

admission – has encountered and been romantically attracted to other women: 'Full many a lady/ I have eyed with best regard'. While this does not necessarily mean his words ought to be considered insincere, it is more likely he is making conscious use of rhetoric reminiscent of that used to woo ladies in the courts of Naples. Conversely, Miranda could be seen to be speaking quite innocently of any agenda: her reference to noble spirits is motivated by having grown up around supernatural beings, not by any knowledge of calculated praise as Ferdinand might be assumed to have. [*AO1 for advancing the argument with a judiciously selected quote; AO2 for the close analysis of the language.*]

- <u>Elsewhere in the play</u>: In Act 5, when Miranda sets eyes on the rest of the coterie from Naples, she again expresses wonderment: 'O brave new world, / That has such people in't!' It is worth noting, however, that this does not derail her affection for Ferdinand: her feelings for him, while perhaps amplified by novelty, transcend it. [*AO1 for advancing the argument with a judiciously selected quote; AO2 for the close analysis of the language.*]

Theme/Paragraph Two: Romantic attraction is borderline obsessive: it causes people to speak in grand, overstated language and Prospero describes it as an 'infection' that has befallen his daughter.

- In the extract above, neither Miranda nor Ferdinand speak in particularly regular iambic pentameter.

Shakespeare frequently overspills the ten syllable count which could be seen as evocative of overwhelming emotion: they simply cannot contain their sentiment to clean verse. When Shakespeare uses ecphonesis in Ferdinand's line 'you, O you', he seems to telegraph that romantic attraction is so overwhelming as to be impossible to confine to mere words, or regulate by the ordinary. Shakespeare thus seems to portray romantic attraction as overwhelming, orderless and frenzied, which is perhaps what Prospero is referring to when he describes Miranda as being '[infected]' by it. [*AO1 for advancing the argument with a judiciously selected quote; AO2 for the close analysis of the language.*]

- In fact, one of the few lines of complete iambic pentameter is the line split between the two lovers: 'of every creature's best/I do not know'. This suggests that a certain clarity seems to come in their union – as though things make more sense and fit more regularly when they join forces. Prospero describes the two lovers as being 'both in either's powers', and perhaps this line is an example of this. [*AO1 for advancing the argument with a judiciously selected quote; AO2 for the close analysis of the language and for discussing how form shapes meaning.*]
- Elsewhere in the play: This sense of frenzy and ethereal compatibility stands in stark contrast to Claribel's feelings towards the Prince of Tunis. Sebastian remarks that she met the match with 'loathness' and that everyone in Alonso's orbit had begged him ('kneel'd to and importuned') not to allow the marriage to go ahead. [*AO1 for advancing the*

argument with a judiciously selected quote; AO2 for
the close analysis of the language.]

**Theme/Paragraph Three: Romantic attraction is
defined in opposition to the carnal attraction that
Caliban expresses towards Miranda.**

- Prospero's abusive treatment of Caliban is largely in
  response to his attempted rape of Miranda. When
  Caliban speaks of Miranda he too notes her beauty;
  but, unlike Ferdinand, almost always qualifies with
  sexual references: 'she will become thy bed' he says to
  Stephano in Act 3 Scene 2. Ferdinand, on the other
  hand, speaks of sex only once to Prospero, in Act 4
  Scene 1, to promise that he shall not break Miranda's
  'virgin knot' before they are married. He assures her
  father that even if he were given 'The most opportune
  place, the strong'st suggestion', it would 'never melt/
  [his] honour into lust'. Those engaged in romantic
  attraction, then, seem to operate under the belief that
  explicit carnality might threaten the sanctity of the
  romance, and seek to exorcise carnal references from
  their lexicon. [*AO1 for advancing the argument with a
  judiciously selected quote; AO2 for the close analysis
  of the language.*]
- Yet though Ferdinand and Miranda wish to remove
  carnal attraction from their romance, it still lurks
  beneath the surface. Shortly after this exchange,
  Miranda obliquely refers to 'what [she] desire[s] to
  give' and 'what [she] shall die to want' – the word 'die'
  a pun on orgasm.[1] Indeed, even this extract hints at a
  suppressed sexuality. When Ferdinand talks of
  Miranda being 'created / Of every creature's best', he

is implicitly breaking her down into her constituent parts: a nod to the blazon tradition, which invites men (and thus the male gaze) to itemise women's physical attributes in a way that arguably sexualises their bodies.[2] Romantic love, then, seeks to suppress carnal feelings, yet it fails to exorcise them altogether. [*AO1 for advancing the argument with a judiciously selected quote; AO2 for the close analysis of the language.*]

Conclusion

'At perhaps the play's most climactic point, as Miranda and Ferdinand are revealed playing chess to Alonso and his coterie, Miranda complains that Ferdinand has cheated in the game: 'Sweet lord, you play me false.' While one may wish to dismiss this as an innocent aside, it in fact points to a darker side of romance: the potential for betrayal or strife – which will become an even greater concern once the lovers leave this isle. That it is a game of chess also seems poignant: after all, it was Prospero's strategic machinations that brought them together. Though these observations do not necessarily undo the other aspects of the pair's romantic attraction – the soaring emotions; the rapture – they do function to remind us of the harsh world in which this romance exists.'

A statue of Shakespeare in Stratford-upon-Avon, the town in which he was born.

At this point in the play, Miranda and Ferdinand, engrossed in a game of chess, have just been revealed to Alonso and his party.

GONZALO

I have inly wept,
Or should have spoke ere this. Look down, you god,
And on this couple drop a blessed crown!
For it is you that have chalk'd forth the way
Which brought us hither.

ALONSO

I say, Amen, Gonzalo!

GONZALO

Was Milan thrust from Milan, that his issue
Should become kings of Naples? O, rejoice
Beyond a common joy, and set it down
With gold on lasting pillars: In one voyage
Did Claribel her husband find at Tunis,
And Ferdinand, her brother, found a wife

Where he himself was lost, Prospero his dukedom
In a poor isle and all of us ourselves
When no man was his own.

Starting with this moment in the play, explore how far Shakespeare Gonzalo as an optimist.

Write about:

• How far Shakespeare presents Gonzalo as an optimist at this moment in the play.

• How far Shakespeare presents Gonzalo as an optimist in the play as a whole.

Introduction

This is a tricky question, because it focuses on a more obscure character; and though such a question is rarer, it is by no means impossible. My advice with such a question is to make sure you are engaging fully with the extract: the examiners will know they have set a tough question, and will have picked a juicy extract to ensure the question is accessible.

"Given that Shakespeare was writing in the wake of the influential sixteenth century Calvinist movement – a theology that implied that God had already determined who would achieve salvation prior to their birth – it is unsurprising that Shakespeare's characters frequently grapple with notions of divine fate and the extent to which it ought to impact their mindset. Gonzalo here seems to posit the existence of a divine plan that assures tidy resolutions: one might hear echoes of Hamlet's assertion that 'there's a special providence in the fall of a sparrow' in his outlook. Yet Gonzalo's optimism extends further: to his view of the island, and how he construes the past."

Theme/Paragraph One: Gonzalo posits the existence of a benevolent divine force that is guiding their lives and assuring positive outcomes.

- Speaking in the wake of a number of revelations – the realisation that both Prospero and Ferdinand are still alive; the discovery of the burgeoning romance between Ferdinand and Miranda – Gonzalo here invokes a divine force ('you god') and asserts that this divine force had assured this seemingly positive turn of events: it had 'chalk'd forth the way / Which brought us hither.' This deeply optimistic conception of the universe – that everything is overseen by a benevolent deity – is seemingly reiterated again when Gonzalo rhetorically summarises the arc of events: 'Was Milan thrust from Milan, that his issue / Should become kings of Naples?' Although framed as a question, it strikes the ear more as a revelation: it is as if God's divine plan – spanning over many years – has finally been revealed, yet had always been assured. The rhyme between 'issue' and 'Naples' – a deliberate orchestration of language on Gonzalo's behalf – mirrors his sense of divine orchestration in the universe. [*AO1 for advancing the argument with a judiciously selected quote; AO2 for the close analysis of the language and for discussing how form shapes meaning.*]

- There is, however, unintentional irony in Gonzalo's use of 'chalk'd'. As a tool for making marks, chalk has an impermanent quality: it can be easily erased and effaced. Shakespeare seems to be undercutting Gonzalo's optimistic view of divinity even as he has Gonzalo articulate it. [*AO1 for advancing the argument with a judiciously selected quote; AO2 for the close analysis of the language.*]

- Elsewhere in the play: Certainly, Gonzalo's optimistic outlook stands in stark contrast to Prospero's. Early in the play, Prospero acknowledges the role of fortune and chance in bringing Alonso and his party to the island: he describes it as an 'accident most strange' and identifies 'Fortune' – as opposed to God – as the driver of these events. That Prospero so openly expresses a chaotic view of the universe only serves to emphasise Gonzalo's ordered, optimistic outlook. [*AO1 for advancing the argument with a judiciously selected quote; AO2 for the close analysis of the language.*]

Theme/Paragraph Two: Gonzalo has a deeply optimistic view of the island and its capacity to bring about positive change.

- Gonzalo in this extract seems to romanticise the island as a kind of engine of positive change: he identifies this 'poor isle' as the entity that not only allowed Prospero to recover 'his dukedom', but also allowed all the other men to achieve a kind of crucial self-discover: it let them find 'all of us ourselves/ When no man was his own.' Whereas to the others in his party the island is a terrifying, menacing place, Gonzalo optimistically sees it as a space that facilitates positive transformation. [*AO1 for advancing the argument with a judiciously selected quote; AO2 for the close analysis of the language.*]

- Elsewhere in the play: Interestingly, Gonzalo appears to have this positive view of the island from the outset. In Act 2 Scene 1, as Gonzalo and the rest of his party are first coming to grips with the space, he seems to conceive of it as an ideal space to play host to a kind of paradise: one in which 'all men.../and women too' would be 'innocent and pure' and 'nature should bring forth.../ ... all abundance.' When Alonso replies that Gonzalo 'speaks nothing to me', one might be reminded of the Greek word *utopia*, which translates to English as 'no-place.' It might also be noted that Gonzalo's utopian vision here in fact reflects a contemporary utopian vision articulated by the French philosopher Michel de Montaigne in his 1580 essay, 'Of the Cannibals,' and which was inspired by observing ways of life that differed from European orthodoxy. [*AO1 for advancing the argument with a judiciously selected quote; AO2 for the close analysis of the language; AO3 for invoking relevant literary context.*]

- Structurally, that Gonzalo expresses this optimistic conception of the island at such a dire point – they have just been shipwrecked; Ferdinand is presumed dead – only accentuates the depths of his optimism. [*AO2 for discussing how form shapes meaning.*]

Theme/Paragraph Three: Gonzalo takes an opti-mistic view of events that have already come to pass. However, there is ambiguity as to whether he is truly optimistic, or whether he wishes to spin events to play the part of dutiful servant.

- In this extract, Gonzalo jarringly conflates Claribel's marriage with the Prince of Tunis and Ferdinand's betrothal to Miranda, framing them as equally fortuitous events: he rhetorically notes that at one and the same time 'did Claribel her husband find at Tunis,/ And Ferdinand, her brother, found a wife.' However, this optimistic reading of Claribel's wedding seems to overlook the acrimony that had accompanied that wedding. In Act 2 Scene 1, Sebastian observes that not only had Claribel met the marriage with 'loathness' and went ahead only out of 'obedience', but also that many in Alonso's orbit had implored him on hands and feet ('kneel'd to') not to force the wedding through. [*AO1 for advancing the argument with a judiciously selected quote; AO2 for the close analysis of the language.*]

- However, while it might be tempting to suggest that Gonzalo's optimism here tips into self-delusion, it is perhaps the case that this particular instance of optimism is a performance that he puts on for Alonso's sake. After Sebastian's observation earlier in the play, for instance, Gonzalo acknowledges that he is speaking truth – 'the truth you speak' – but protests that he 'lack[s] some gentleness, / And time to speak it in.' Indeed, even in this extract there are subtle hints that his optimism about Claribel's wedding is something of a facade: the line 'did Claribel her husband find at Tunis' ends with an unstressed hyperbeat that oversteps the iambic pentameter, as it gestures to the fact that the marriage was not such a tidy fit after all.[1] [*AO1 for advancing the argument with a judiciously selected quote; AO2 for the close analysis of the language and for discussing how form shapes meaning.*]

Conclusion

"When Prospero and Miranda – following Antonio's coup – were ejected from Milan, Prospero notes that Gonzalo had secretly furnished them with 'linens, stuffs and necessaries:' a deeply optimistic course of action, given that Prospero and Miranda were set off to sea in a mere 'rotten carcass of a boat' with a slim chance of survival. Yet while it is tempting to dub Gonzalo as naively optimistic, he is in fact a more complicated figure: at times affecting optimism as a means to bolster others psychologically – thus a self-conscious counterpoint to the cynicism embodied by Sebastian and Antonio."

Street art rendering of Shakespeare in London

ENDNOTES

ESSAY PLAN ONE

1. A patriarchy is a society ruled by men. A patriarchal figure is therefore a man in a position of power.
2. Shakespeare's plays are almost entirely written in *iambic pentameter*. An iamb is a metrical foot in which the emphasis is on the second syllable, and tends to sound more like natural speech. A pentameter is when there are five metrical feet in a line.

   It is often easiest to illustrate with an example. If we take the first line of Prospero's speech here, and use bold font to represent the stressed syllables, plus a vertical bar to indicate the end of each metrical foot, it will look like this: 'To **have** | no **screen** | be**tween** | this **part** | he **play'd**.' Since there are five metrical feet here, all iambic, it is rendered in iambic pentameter.

   However, if we look at the line I've cited, we can see that it contains more than ten syllables – 'Mark **his** | con**di** | tion **and** | the e | **vent**; then | **tell me**' – and thus overspills the iambic pentameter that usually characterises Prospero's speech.

   In fact, there are other interesting things going on here. The fourth metrical foot contains two unstressed syllables – this is called a pyrrhic foot. The fifth foot has a stress on the first syllable, but not the second syllable – this is called a trochaic foot.
3. A character's machinations refers to their plans and their attempts to implement them.

   To transgress is to go beyond or exceed what is permissible.
4. The setup at the start of *Hamlet* is that Hamlet's father – the King – has been murdered by Hamlet's uncle, Claudius, and Claudius has seized the throne. The plot revolves around Hamlet's efforts to avenge his murdered father.
5. To eschew something is to reject it.
6. A matriarch is a woman in a position of power. Although Shakespeare's England was a patriarchal society, matriarchal figures could still exist – though their power was almost always lesser than society's patriarchal figures.
7. To be subservient to someone is to be in a position in which you serve them and/or acknowledge their power over you.
8. Fraternal love is the love between brothers.
9. To be a surrogate father is to be a stand-in or substitution for a father.

10. The word "Freudian" refers to the father of psychoanalysis, Sigmund Freud (1856 – 1939). His works explore the hidden sexual motivations that drive human beings. When we are doing a Freudian reading of a text, we are looking for the hidden sexual or taboo imagery – imagery that perhaps even the author themselves had not realized possessed sexual/taboo undertones. In this instance, the crime Caliban tried to commit – rape – is already sexual in nature and taboo. However, the *hidden* taboo is that Miranda is in a sense his sister.

If you are levelling opprobrium at something it means you are harshly critical of it.

ESSAY PLAN TWO

1. To be equivocal about something is to have a split, even contradictory opinion about it.
2. To be verbose is to use more words – and longer words – than is necessary. Enjambment is when a sentence runs over multiple lines of poetry.
3. To have paternal pride is to have fatherly pride.
4. To be in someone's thrall is to be under their power.
5. Realpolitik refers to a style of doing politics that puts the securement and reconciliation of power over and above all other concerns, be they moral or social.
6. To abdicate power is to give up power.

ESSAY PLAN THREE

1. Literalisation refers to the process of taking something that would otherwise be metaphorical, and making it literally the case. The adage 'knowledge is power' is metaphorical. However, Prospero is given literal power through his magic.
2. 'Cum' in 'scholar-cum-magician' is a Latin phrase. It is usually used to describe two characteristics about a certain individual – for example, Barack Obama is a lawyer-cum-politician.

   In Geoffrey Chaucer's *The Franklin's Tale* – which was part of *The Canterbury Tales*, a text Shakespeare would have been familiar with – a young knight called Aurelius visits this magician-cum-scholar because he wants the magician to use his magic to alter the natural landscape and submerge the black rocks that populate the coast.
3. Caesura is when you have a piece of punctuation midway through a line of poetry. The phrase 'structural parallelism' points to the fact that the same word appears twice, either side of the caesura.

   Monosyllabism refers to the use of single syllable words to achieve a certain effect.
4. A polysyllabic word is a one that contains a number of syllables.

5. Consonance is when the same – or very similar – constantans are repeated in quick succession.
6. A paradox is when you have two contradictory ideas in tandem: for instance, that education is the path to power, but is also something that threatens to undercut someone's power. Another example of a paradox is the idea that God might make a stone so heavy that even he could not move it. The immovability of the stone clashes with the idea of God as an infinitely powerful being.
7. A catalyst for an event is something that kicks that event into action.
8. The word eponymous basically means that the main character in the play has the same name as the play's title.
   If something is in a state of stasis, it means it is completely still.

ESSAY PLAN FOUR

1. To usurp power from someone is to forcibly take power from them.
2. Anacoluthon refers to a sentence which breaks down in coherence halfway through, and then starts suddenly moving onto something else. It often is characterized by an abrupt use of harsh punctuation midway through the sentence.
3. Zeus is the god of the sky and thunder in Greek mythology. A deity is a kind of god.
4. Dramatis Personae is a Latin phrase and refers to the characters who appear in a play or novel.

ESSAY PLAN FIVE

1. Anaphora is when you have a word or phrase repeated at the start of a number of clauses in a row. In this case, the word that is being repeated is: 'I'll.'
2. To be obsequious is to be obliging in a slavish, over-the-top way.

ESSAY PLAN SIX

1. Obliquely means indirectly. So to bring something up obliquely means to bring it up in a roundabout way.
   In the Elizabethan/Jacobean era, 'die' was slang for 'orgasm.'
2. Blazon is a form of poetry in which a male speaker itemises a woman's physical attributes. The phrase 'male gaze' comes from feminist theory, and refers to the way in which men – particularly heterosexual men – view the world.

ESSAY PLAN SEVEN

1. What, I hear you ask, is an unstressed hyperbeat?

   Let's take a closer look at this line: 'Did **Cla** | ri**bel** | her **hus**| band **find** | at **Tu** | nis.' We have five iambs in a row; but we then have one final syllable at the end. Since it an unstressed syllable, we call it an unstressed hyperbeat – or a feminine ending. If it had been stressed, we would call it a stressed hyperbeat – or a masculine ending.

ENGLISH LANGUAGE

English Language Paper One: A Technique Guide for GCSE (9-1)

English Language Paper Two : A Technique Guide for GCSE (9-1)

If you found this book useful, please consider leaving a review on Amazon, which you can do at the following link: **https://rcl.ink/rfMbH**

You can also join our private Facebook group (where our authors share resources and guidance) by visiting the following link: **https://rcl.ink/DME.**

Printed in Great Britain
by Amazon

64680447R00047